LOW CARB YOUR WAY TO THE PERFECT BODY

Cut The Calories Cut The Fat

DIANA WATSON

Copyright © 2017 Diana Watson
All rights reserved

TABLE OF CONTENTS

LOW CARB YOUR WAY TO THE PERFECT BODY
Cut The Calories
Cut The Fat
INTRODUCTION
PERKS OF LOW CARB
STOCKING YOUR PANTRY
BREAKFAST
BUNLESS BACON, EGG, AND CHEESE
EGGS WITH TOMATOES AND SCALLIONS
BROCCOLI AND CHEESE OMELET
FETA AND SPINACH FRITTATA
POACHED EGGS WITH ASPARAGUS
EGG-IN-A-HOLE
BAKED EGGS IN SPINACH
MAIN DISHES
CHICKEN FAJITA BOWLS
STEAK TACO SALAD
MUSSELS IN BASIL SAUCE
GARLIC LEMON TILAPIA
CHICKEN WITH ARTICHOKE AND FETA
PORK CHOPS WITH MUSHROOMS
THAI CURRY SHRIMP
SIDES AND SNACKS
LOADED CAULIFLOWER BITES
HASSELBACK ZUCCHINI
DEVILED EGGS
AUTUMN SALAD WITH GORGONZOLA AND PEARS
ROASTED BROCCOLI WITH GARLIC
SPAGHETTI SQUASH PESTO
PUMPKIN SEEDS
DESSERTS
OVEN-BAKED BRIE CHEESE
PINEAPPLE ZUCCHINI CAKE
CINNAMON APPLES WITH VANILLA SAUCE
CRUNCHY BERRY MOUSSE
LOW-CARB CHOCOLATE MOUSSE
SALTY CHOCOLATE TREAT

CREAMY COTTAGE CHEESE PUDDING
CONCLUSION
INTRODUCTION
UNDERSTAND THE RESISTANCE
INSULIN RESISTANCE DIET
LONG-TERM MANAGEMENT
DIET PLAN
RECIPES
Chapter 1: The Power of the Crock Pot and Its Benefits
Chapter 2: Healthy Breakfast Recipes
Boiled Eggs
One-Hour Bread

INTRODUCTION

Congratulations on purchasing your personal copy of *The Ultimate Low Carb Cookbook.* Thank you for doing so.

The following chapters will provide with information and recipes so that you can get started on your low carb diet journey today.

There are plenty of books on this subject on the market, thanks again for choosing this one! Every effort was made to ensure it is full of as much useful information as possible. Please enjoy!

PERKS OF LOW CARB

Why in the world should you eat fewer carbs? There are many benefits for people of all ages.

Here are some of the main benefits of a low carb diet:

- Weight loss
- Reversing your Type 2 Diabetes
- Help Stomach Ailments
- Fewer Sugar Cravings
- Help with Blood Pressure
- Less Acne
- More Energy
- Help with Epilepsy
- Help with Heartburn
- Reverse PCOS

- Reduce ADHD Symptoms

- Staying away from carbs can result in weight loss without feeling hungry.

- Low carb weight loss has been used for about 150 years, and it is more effective than other diets

- Why does it work and how can the effects be maximized?

- It is not a coincidence that staying away from carbohydrates like bread and sugar has special benefits beyond the calories. Carbs cause your body to release insulin. Insulin is the body's fat-storing hormone.

- To be able to lose excess body fat, your first goal is reducing insulin levels. You do this by eating fewer carbs. For a lot of people, this will help them reach their weight loss goals.

- Weight loss is simply thought of as just

calories – eat fewer calories, burn more calories, and you will lose weight. While this is true in theory, it is not useful practically as shown by an obesity epidemic during the time when people believed this.

- The main problem with just focusing on calories is it ignores hunger. It ignores the body's regulation of the fat is has stored. It ignores that if we don't eat calories, we eat food. Food is much more than just calories. Low carb foods will make you feel full. Other foods like soda will make you feel even more hungry.

- The idea of low carbs is to work with the body, not against it. Don't waste time and willpower on restricting calories, enduring hunger, and exercising - we need to do something else. We make our bodies want to eat less, and it will burn more of any excess we have.

- It does this by altering our hormonal balance. One hormone is most instrumental in doing this, and that is the fat-storing hormone insulin.

- Lowering insulin will increase fat burning, and this enables the body to release stored up body fat. This will result in less hunger and increased energy without exercising.

-

- ## STOCKING YOUR PANTRY

- Want to know what you can eat? What to stay away from? What can you indulge in now and then? Stock up on essentials and never buy what you don't need.

- When you start eating low-carb whole foods, there will be less food in your pantry since you will be buying less processed foods. You will be shopping the outer perimeters of the store for fresh fruits and vegetables, fish and meat, cheese and milk. Stay away from the inner aisles that hold all the processed foods.

- You might be wondering if it will cost more to eat low carb, but it is cheaper. You won't be buying chocolate, sweet treats, sugar, flour, rolls, wraps, bread, and junk food. Utilize the store's specials to find fruits and vegetables on sale. You might also find specials on meats.

- You will spend more money on good quality ingredients, but you will be shopping less. Anything you spend is an investment in your family and their health.

- You will also be saving money on taking out foods. One night's take out meal could easily add up to the same as feeding a family for a few days on healthy food.

- Check labels for fat and carb content as different brands can vary. Read every label on all the products you buy. It can be an eye-opener. You will learn what brands that are safe to buy and what to stay away from. Tuna might be packed with wheat and sugar; others are packed in olive oil.

- Healthy foods can have sugars added to them. When figuring out recipes, make sure you have picked the correct brand of food that you are using since nutritional values could vary. To figure out net carbs just subtract the fiber from the total carb value.

- Below you will find a shopping list:

- **Sauces and Flavorings**

- Full-fat mayonnaise

- Vinegars

- Fresh herbs

- Spices and herbs

- Himalayan salt

- **Pantry Ingredients**

- Almond meal and flour

- Sugar-free jelly

- Coconut shredded, unsweetened

- Cocoa

- Stevia, erythritol
- Coconut flour
- Ground almonds
- Nuts and seeds – stay away from cashews and peanuts
- Canned tomatoes
- Olives, stuffed or black

- **Fats and Oils**

  - Stay away from seed oils like omega 6, canola, sunflower
  - Macadamia oil
  - Coconut oil
  - Butter
  - Olive oil
  - Avocado oil

- **Dairy**

- Sour cream
- Haloumi
- Feta
- Full fat cream cheese
- Cream
- Full fat yogurt
- All types of cheeses
- **Fridge**
- Eggs – you can eat these any way you like – scrambled, omelet, fried, boiled, etc.
- Fish – sardines, tuna, hoki, mussels, shrimp - fresh and frozen, snapper, salmon, all fatty omega-3 rich seafood. Stay away from crumbled or battered fish.
- Lean meats
- Sausages – check labels to make sure it has high meat content without fillers.

- Chicken
- Bacon – no honey cured, or sugar added
- Free range or grass fed meats
- Ingredients for salads
- Fruits
- Vegetables except for root vegetables like potatoes, parsnips, carrots, etc.

- # BREAKFAST

- BUNLESS BACON, EGG, AND CHEESE
- Serves: 1
- Ingredients:
- ¼ c shredded cheese
- 2 slices bacon, cooked
- ½ avocado, mashed
- 2 tbsp water
- 2 eggs

- Instructions:
- Place two Mason jar rings in a skillet. Spray everything with nonstick spray. Crack an egg into each of the lids and break up the yoke with a fork
- Pour the water into the skillet and place the lid on the skillet. Let the eggs steam for three minutes. Place cheese on one of the eggs, let cook until cheese melts.
- Place the egg, without the cheese, onto a plate. Add bacon and avocado. Place cheesy egg, cheese-side-down on top.
-

-
- EGGS WITH TOMATOES AND SCALLIONS
- Serves: 2
- Ingredients:
- Pepper and salt
- 1 tsp olive oil
- 1 large tomato, diced
- 4 scallions, diced
- 3 egg whites
- 2 eggs
- Instructions:
- Place oil in a skillet and heat. Mix in the tomatoes and scallions. Beat the eggs, pepper, and salt together. Pour the eggs into the skillet and scramble until done.
-

- BROCCOLI AND CHEESE OMELET
- Serves: 1
- Ingredients:
- Slice Swiss cheese
- ½ c broccoli, cooked
- Nonstick spray
- Pepper and salt
- 1 tbsp skim milk
- 2 egg whites
- 1 egg
- Instructions:
- Beat together pepper, salt, milk, and eggs. Heat a pan and spray with nonstick spray. Once warm, pour in the eggs a rotate to cover the bottom. Lower heat.
- Place the cheese down the center a top with

broccoli. Once the egg is cooked, flip the edges over the fillings.

-
- FETA AND SPINACH FRITTATA
- Serves: 4
- Ingredients:
- Pepper and salt
- 2 tbsp grated Parmigiano-Reggiano
- 2-oz feta crumbled
- 10-oz thawed frozen spinach
- 3 chopped scallions
- ½ red onion, chopped
- 1 tsp olive oil
- 8 egg whites
- 2 eggs
- Instructions:
- Remove all water from the spinach.
- Heat the oil in a non-stick skillet.

- Place in the scallions and onion and cook four minutes, or until soft.
- Beat the eggs together and mix in spinach, cheeses, pepper, and salt.
- Pour into the hot skillet and let it cook for about five minutes, or until the bottom is set.
- Flip your frittata over in a manner that is most comfortable to you, and allow the other side to cook through.
- POACHED EGGS WITH ASPARAGUS
- Serves: 4
- Ingredients:
- 2 tbsp Parmigiano Reggiano
- Pepper and salt
- 4 eggs
- 2 bunches asparagus, ends removed
- Instructions:

- Steam the asparagus until they are tender-crisp, and then run under cool water to stop the cooking. Drain and place onto four different plates.

- Poach each egg. Take them out with a slotted spoon and place an egg on top of each asparagus bunch. Top with the cheese, pepper, and salt.

-

-
- EGG-IN-A-HOLE
- Serves: 4
- Ingredients:
- Pepper and salt
- 4 eggs
- 1 bell pepper, sliced in 4 ½ in rings
- Nonstick spray
- Instructions:
- Heat up a skillet and spray with nonstick spray. Place in the pepper and allow it to cook for a minute. Crack an egg into each pepper ring and season with pepper and salt. Allow to cook until the eggs are done to your liking. Two to three minutes will bring the eggs to runny.
-

BAKED EGGS IN SPINACH

Serves: 4

Ingredients:

- Nonstick spray
- 2 tbsp asiago cheese
- Pepper and salt
- 4 eggs
- 1 ½ lb baby spinach
- ¼ c shallots, diced
- 2 tsp olive oil

Instructions:

- Your oven should be set to 400. Spray four small oven-safe dishes with nonstick spray.
- Add oil to a pan and heat. Add in the shallots and cook for two to three minutes. Mix in the pepper, salt, and spinach, cooking until wilted.

Stir in the asiago.

- Divide the spinach between the dishes and form and well in the center. Crack an egg into each and top with pepper and salt. Place the dishes on baking sheets and cook about 17 minutes or until the yolks are set to your liking.

-

-

- MAIN DISHES

- CHICKEN FAJITA BOWLS

- Serves: 4

- Ingredients:

- 2 tbsp lime juice

- 2 tsp cumin

- 24-oz bag riced cauliflower

- 1 tsp salt

- 1 tsp garlic powder

- 1/3 c cilantro, chopped

- 2 tsp paprika

- 2 tbsp EVOO

- 1 sweet onion, sliced

- 3 bell peppers, sliced

- 2 tsp chili powder
- 1 lb chicken breasts, boneless skinless
- Instructions:
- Your oven should be at 400. Put the chicken on half of a baking sheet and the onions and peppers on the other. Drizzle everything with olive oil.
- Mix the salt, garlic, cumin, paprika, and chili powder together. Sprinkle over the veggies and chicken. Make sure that you toss the veggies and flip the chicken so that everything is coated. Bake for 20 minutes.
- Meanwhile, cook the cauliflower as the bag says to. After finished, toss with lime juice and cilantro. Serve everything together and top with avocado, sour cream, or cheese.
-

- STEAK TACO SALAD
- Serves: 4
- Ingredients:
- 2 sliced green onions
- 1 tsp oregano
- 1 c halved cherry tomatoes
- 1 c black beans, drained and rinsed
- 1 romaine head, chopped
- Salt
- 1 c corn
- 1 tsp cumin
- 2 limes, juiced
- 1 tbsp taco seasoning
- ¾ lb steak
- ¼ c + 1 tbsp EVOO, divided

- Instructions:

- Heat a tablespoon of oil in a pan. Coat the steak with the taco seasoning. Cook until it is cooked to your liking, flip only once. Place on a cutting board and allow to rest for five minutes; slice against the grain.

- As the steak cooks, make the dressing. Whisk the oregano, cumin, lime juice, and the rest of the oil together, and then season with salt.

- In a large bowl, add in the onion, tomatoes, beans, corn, steak, and romaine. Season with salt and top with dressing.

-

-
- MUSSELS IN BASIL SAUCE
- Serves: 3
- Ingredients:
- Pepper and salt
- ¼ c parmesan
- 2 tbsp olive oil
- ½ c basil
- ½ c half and half, fat-free
- ½ c white wine
- 2 garlic cloves
- 1 garlic clove, smashed a chopped
- 1 shallot, minced
- 2 tsp butter
- Instructions:
- De-bread and scrub your mussels in cold water. Get rid of any cracked shells. Using a

large pot, melt the butter. Place in the chopped garlic and shallots and sauté for about three minutes. Pour in the wine and allow to boil. Place in the mussels and top with the lid Allow cooking four to six minutes until the mussels open. Once cooked, remove from the pot with a slotted spoon. Get rid of any that didn't open.

- Add ¼ of a cup of half and half to the pot and let simmer for four minutes.

- Place the rest of the garlic, half and half, olive oil, parmesan, and basil in a blender and puree. Pour into the pot and add pepper and salt. Let simmer a few minutes long then serve over top of the mussels.

-

- GARLIC LEMON TILAPIA

- Serves: 6

- Ingredients:

- Nonstick spray

- 2 tbsp butter

- Pepper and salt

- 4 tsp parsley

- 2 tbsp lemon juice

- 4 crushed garlic cloves

- 6 6-oz tilapia filets

- Instructions:

- Your oven should be set to 400.

- Melt the butter in a small skillet. Cook the garlic for a minute. Mix in the lemon juice and turn off the heat.

- Coat a casserole dish with nonstick spray.

- Put the fish in the dish and season with pepper and salt. Pour the butter mixture over the fish and then sprinkle with the parsley.

- Cook for about 15 minutes.

CHICKEN WITH ARTICHOKE AND FETA

Serves: 6

Ingredients:

- Pepper and salt
- 2 tbsp parsley, chopped
- ¼ c feta cheese, reduced-fat
- 1 tsp oregano
- 1 crushed garlic clove
- 6-oz jar artichoke hearts
- 6 chicken thighs, boneless and skinless

Instructions:

- Place the artichoke hearts, and their juice, in a bag with the chicken. Allow them to marinate at least 20 minutes. Drain the liquid and mix in the pepper, salt, oregano, and garlic.
- Broil the chicken for about ten minutes. Flip

the chicken and cook another eight to ten minutes, or until fully cooked. Top with the feta and cook long enough to melt. Serve with fresh parsley.

-
- PORK CHOPS WITH MUSHROOMS
- Serves: 4
- Ingredients:
- 2 tbsp parsley, chopped
- 1 tbsp Dijon
- 10-oz baby Bella mushrooms, sliced
- 1 c chicken stock, low-sodium
- ¼ c shallots, chopped
- Pepper
- ½ tsp salt
- 4 pork chops, bone-in
- 1 tsp ghee
- Instructions:
- Melt the ghee in a large skillet. Top with pepper and salt on both sides of all the pork chops. Sauté the chops in the skillet for seven

minutes, flip, and cook for another seven minutes. The thermometer should red 160F. Remove the pork and keep warm.

- Place the shallots in the pan and cook for about three minutes. Pour in the stock and deglaze the pan. Mix in the pepper, mushrooms, one tablespoon parsley, and mustard. Cook for about three minutes. Serve the chops topped with the gravy and sprinkle with the remaining parsley.

-

- THAI CURRY SHRIMP

- Serves: 4

- Ingredients:

- Salt

- 2 tbsp basil, chopped

- 2 tsp Thai fish sauce

- 6-oz coconut milk

- 1 lb shrimp, cleaned

- 2 minced garlic cloves

- 1 tbsp Thai green curry paste

- 4 scallions, chopped

- 1 tsp oil

- Instructions:

- Heat oil in a large skillet. Place in the white parts of the scallion and curry paste. Cook for a minute.

- Mix in the salt, garlic, and shrimp. Cook for another two to three minutes.

- Pour in the fish sauce and coconut milk. Simmer for two to three minutes, or until the shrimp is fully cooked.

- Take it off the heat and mix in the basil and scallion greens. Serve with basmati rice.

-

SIDES AND SNACKS

- LOADED CAULIFLOWER BITES
- Serves: 6
- Ingredients:
- 1 tbsp chives, chopped
- 5 bacon slices, cooked and crumbled
- 1 c shredded cheese
- 1 tsp garlic powder
- Pepper
- Salt
- 2 tbsp EVOO
- 1 head cauliflower, cut into florets
- Cooking spray
- Instructions:

- Your oven should be at 425. Spray a baking sheet with nonstick spray.
- Bring salted water to a boil and cook the cauliflower for about five minutes, and then drain.
- Spread them on the baking sheet and coat with the garlic, pepper, salt, and oil. With a potato masher or glass, smash the florets.
- Top each smash with some bacon, and cheese. Bake for about 15 minutes. Sprinkle them with chives.
- HASSELBACK ZUCCHINI
- Serves: 4
- Ingredients:
- ¼ tsp red pepper flakes
- Salt
- ¼ c parmesan

- 3 tbsp EVOO
- 1 lb zucchini, ends cut off
- Instructions:
- Your oven should be at 400. Cut slices into the zucchini making sure not to cut all the way through. Using two wooden spoons as guides can help.
- Drizzle with the oil and season with the red pepper flakes, salt, and parmesan.
- Cook for about 25 minutes. It should be golden and tender.

- DEVILED EGGS
- Serves: 4
- Ingredients:
- 2 tbsp chives, chopped
- Pepper and salt
- Paprika
- 1 tsp Dijon
- 2 tbsp light mayo
- 4 hard boiled eggs, cooled and peeled
- Instructions:
- Slice the eggs long-ways. Remove the yolks and place them in a small bowl. Mix in the pepper, salt, mustard, and mayo. Mix well and place them in a piping bad. Pipe the mixture into the egg white and top with paprika and chives.

•

-
- AUTUMN SALAD WITH GORGONZOLA AND PEARS
- Serves: 6
- Ingredients:
- Dressing:
- 3 tbsp olive oil
- Pepper
- ¼ tsp salt
- 1 tsp honey
- ½ tsp Dijon
- 2 tbsp red wine vinegar
- Salad:
- 1-oz pecans
- 8-oz mixed baby greens
- ¼ c gorgonzola cheese, crumbled
- 2 small ripe pears, diced and peeled

- Instructions:
- Mix the pepper, salt, honey, mustard, and vinegar together. Whisk in the oil until it all comes together.
- Combine all of the salad ingredients together. Once you are ready to serve, top with the vinaigrette and toss.
- ROASTED BROCCOLI WITH GARLIC
- Serves: 4
- Ingredients:
- Pepper and salt
- 2 tbsp EVOO
- 6 smashed garlic cloves
- 1 ½ lb broccoli florets
- Instructions:
- Your oven should be set at 450. In your baking dish, mix the pepper, salt, garlic, olive oil, and

broccoli. Cook for about 20 minutes. The broccoli should be tender and brown.

-

- SPAGHETTI SQUASH PESTO

- Serves: 4

- Ingredients:

- 1 tomato, diced

- Pepper and salt

- 3 tbsp Parmigiano-Reggiano

- ¼ c olive oil

- 1 small garlic clove

- 15 basil leaves

- 1 small spaghetti squash

- Instructions:

- Slice the squash in half and scoop out seeds and fibers. Place the squash in a microwaveable dish and cover. Microwave for eight to nine minutes. Take out of the microwave and scoop out the flesh with a fork, and place in a large bowl.

- In a blender, mix the pepper, salt, cheese, olive oil, garlic, and basil until smooth.

- Mix two cups spaghetti squash with the pesto and toss in the pepper, salt, and tomatoes.

-
- PUMPKIN SEEDS
- Serves: varies
- Ingredients:
- Salt
- Olive oil spray
- Pumpkin seeds
- Instructions:
- Clean the pumpkin seeds.
- Spread the seeds on a baking sheet and let it dry overnight.
- Your oven should be set to 250. Lightly coat the seeds with cooking spray or oil and sprinkle with as much salt as you like
- Cook them until they turn golden. This should take about an hour and fifteen minutes.
- Allow to cool and enjoy.

-
-

-
- DESSERTS
-
- OVEN-BAKED BRIE CHEESE
- Serves: 4
- Ingredients:
- 1 tbsp olive oil
- Pepper and salt
- 1 tbsp rosemary
- 1 garlic clove
- 2-oz pecan
- 8 ¾-oz Brie
- Instructions:
- Your oven should be at 400. Place parchment paper on a baking sheet and lay the cheese on top.
- Chop the herbs and nuts and mince the garlic.

Mix them together with the olive oil and season with pepper and salt. Place the mixture on the cheese and cook for ten minutes.

-

-
- PINEAPPLE ZUCCHINI CAKE
- Serves: 16
- Ingredients:
- Cake:
- 20-oz crushed pineapple, drained
- 2 c zucchini, grated
- 1 tsp vanilla
- 2 eggs
- 3 tbsp canola oil
- 1 tsp salt
- Pinch ginger
- ¼ tsp nutmeg
- 2 tsp cinnamon
- 2 tsp baking soda
- 1 c sugar

- ¾ c whole wheat flour
- ¾ c AP flour
- ½ c coconut, flaked
- Frosting:
- 1 tsp vanilla
- 1 c powdered sugar
- 8-oz 1/3 fat cream cheese
- Instructions:
- Your oven should be set to 350. Mix the spices, salt, baking soda, coconut, sugar, and flours.
- Mix the vanilla, eggs, and oil together. Stir in the pineapple and zucchini. Fold the wet into the dry ingredients. It will start out dry and stiff but continue to mix; it will eventually come together.
- Coat a Bundt pan with cooking spray and spoon in the batter. Bake for 33 to 40 minutes.

Let the cake cool on wire rack completely before frosting.

- For the frosting: beat all of the frosting ingredients together. Spread the frosting on the cake and top with chopped pecans if you want.

-
- CINNAMON APPLES WITH VANILLA SAUCE
- Serves: 6
- Ingredients:
- Sauce:
- 2 c heavy cream
- 1 egg yolk
- 2 tbsp butter
- 1 star anise
- ½ tsp vanilla
- 8 tbsp heavy cream
- Apples:
- 1 tsp cinnamon
- 3 apples, preferably tart and firm
- 3 tbsp butter
- Instructions:

- Bring the eight tablespoons of heavy cream, star anise, vanilla, and butter to a boil. Turn the heat down and allow to simmer for five minutes. It should turn creamy.
- Take it off the heat and take out the star anise. Mix in the yolk and whisk vigorously. Allow the mixture to cool completely
- Whisk the 2 cups of heavy cream with the completely cold cream mix.
- Let the mixture refrigerate for 30 minutes.
- Wash, core, and slice the apples. Melt the butter in a skillet and brown up the apple slices. Mix in the cinnamon until almost done.
- Serve the apples topped with the vanilla sauce.
-

- CRUNCHY BERRY MOUSSE
- Serves: 8
- Ingredients:
- ¼ tsp vanilla
- ½ lemon, zested
- 1 ¾ oz chopped pecans
- 3 ¼ oz mixed berries
- 2 c heavy cream
- Instructions:
- Place the cream in a bowl and whip until soft peaks begin to form. Mix in the vanilla and lemon zest.
- Gently fold in the nuts and berries.
- Top the bowl with cling wrap and refrigerate the mixture for at least three hours, or until the mixture has firmed into a mousse. If you

don't mind a less firm consistency, then you can enjoy it immediately.

-

-
- LOW-CARB CHOCOLATE MOUSSE
- Serves: 6
- Ingredients:
- 3 1/3 c coconut milk
- 2 to 3 tbsp. cocoa powder
- 1 tsp. vanilla extract
- 1 tsp. honey
- Instructions:
- Put coconut milk in the fridge for four hours until the cream separates from the water.
- Open can carefully and spoon out the cream and place in a bowl. Keep the coconut water for pancakes or smoothies.
- Whisk the cream, vanilla, and honey with a hand mixer until thick. Add cocoa and whisk more.

- Serve in dessert bowls.

- If you place the mousse in the freezer for about an hour, you will have ice cream.

-

-
- SALTY CHOCOLATE TREAT
- Serves: 10
- Ingredients:
- 3 ½ oz. dark chocolate, minimum of 70 % cocoa
- 10 hazelnuts, walnuts, or pecans
- 2 tbsp. roasted unsweet coconut chips
- 1 tbsp. pumpkin seeds
- Sea salt
- Instructions:
- Melt chocolate. Have 10 small cupcake liner. No bigger than 2 inches.
- Put melted chocolate into the liners.
- Add seeds, coconut chips, and nuts. Sprinkle with salt.

- Allow to cool and store in the fridge.

- If you don't have cupcake liners, you can pour the chocolate into a small dish lined with parchment paper about 8 x 8 inches. Place coconut, nuts, and sea salt onto chocolate before it is completely hard. Once completely hardened, break up into pieces. You could add chili for flavor or some dry berries such as goji or blueberries if you are not sensitive to sugar.

-

- CREAMY COTTAGE CHEESE PUDDING
- Serves: 6
- Ingredients:
- 2/3 lbs. cottage cheese
- 1 ¼ c heavy whipping cream
- 1 tsp vanilla extract
- 1 tsp ground cinnamon
- 2 oz. fresh raspberries or berry of choice
- Instructions:
- Whip heavy cream until it forms soft peaks. Add vanilla. Mix in cinnamon or sprinkle on top before serving.
- Gently fold in cottage cheese. Do not over mix. Let pudding sit in fridge about 10 to 15 minutes.

- Serve with red berries of choice either mashed or whole. Wedges of oranges or Clementine are delicious as well.

-

-

-

-

- ## CONCLUSION

- Thank for making it through to the end of *The Ultimate Low Carb Cookbook.* Let's hope it was informative and able to provide you with all of the tools you need to achieve your goals.

- Now you have plenty of recipes to get you started on your weight loss journey. You have all the information you need, and the recipes to get you started, so start today.

BOOK TWO

INSULIN RESISTANCE DIET PLAN FOR TYPE 2 DIABETICS

DIANA WATSON

TABLE OF CONTENTS

- LOW CARB YOUR WAY TO THE PERFECT BODY
- *Cut The Calories*
- *Cut The Fat*
- INTRODUCTION
- PERKS OF LOW CARB
- STOCKING YOUR PANTRY
- BREAKFAST
- BUNLESS BACON, EGG, AND CHEESE
- EGGS WITH TOMATOES AND SCALLIONS
- BROCCOLI AND CHEESE OMELET
- FETA AND SPINACH FRITTATA
- POACHED EGGS WITH ASPARAGUS
- EGG-IN-A-HOLE
- BAKED EGGS IN SPINACH
- MAIN DISHES
- CHICKEN FAJITA BOWLS
- STEAK TACO SALAD
- MUSSELS IN BASIL SAUCE
- GARLIC LEMON TILAPIA
- CHICKEN WITH ARTICHOKE AND FETA
- PORK CHOPS WITH MUSHROOMS
- THAI CURRY SHRIMP
- SIDES AND SNACKS
- LOADED CAULIFLOWER BITES
- HASSELBACK ZUCCHINI
- DEVILED EGGS
- AUTUMN SALAD WITH GORGONZOLA AND PEARS
- ROASTED BROCCOLI WITH GARLIC
- SPAGHETTI SQUASH PESTO
- PUMPKIN SEEDS
- DESSERTS
- OVEN-BAKED BRIE CHEESE
- PINEAPPLE ZUCCHINI CAKE

- CINNAMON APPLES WITH VANILLA SAUCE
- CRUNCHY BERRY MOUSSE
- LOW-CARB CHOCOLATE MOUSSE
- SALTY CHOCOLATE TREAT
- CREAMY COTTAGE CHEESE PUDDING
- CONCLUSION
- INTRODUCTION
- UNDERSTAND THE RESISTANCE
- INSULIN RESISTANCE DIET
- LONG-TERM MANAGEMENT
- DIET PLAN
- RECIPES
- Chapter 1: The Power of the Crock Pot and Its Benefits
- Chapter 2: Healthy Breakfast Recipes
- Boiled Eggs
- One-Hour Bread
-
-
-
-

- **VIP Subscriber List**
- Hi Dear Reader, this is Diana! If you like my book and you want to receive the latest tips and tricks on cooking, weight-loss, cookbook recipes and more, do [subscribe to my mailing list in the link here](#)! I will then be able to send you the most up-to-date information about my upcoming books and promotions as well! [Thank you for supporting my work and happy reading!](#)

INTRODUCTION

- Congratulations on purchasing your personal copy of *Insulin Resistance Diet Plan for Type 2 Diabetics.* Thank you for doing so.
- If you find you are being warned by your doctor that you are at high risk of developing diabetes, or that you have insulin resistance, you're not alone. In fact, it's believed that the

number of diabetics is going to double from around 190 million to 325 million within the next couple of decades. A study performed in 2002 found that 32.2% of the population in the US are insulin resistant.

- Knowing how insulin resistance works on a cellular level helps people know the best ways to treat and prevent type 2 diabetes. Individuals who suffer from diabetes mellitus and obese people are often insulin resistant. Many studies have discovered that an insulin resistance diet and exercise can alter the pathways and slow down the onset of insulin resistance.
- It's safe to say that if we look at ways to change our habits, and pay attention to what we do, we can make some improvements to our life. An insulin resistance diet can help you to lose weight and will turn regulate your

blood glucose and insulin levels so that your chances of developing diabetes are lowered.
- It's possible that insulin resistance is the leading cause of many of today's chronic diseases. These diseases are collectively killing over a million people each year. The good thing is that it can easily be improved with some simple changed in your eating, lifestyle, and exercise habits. Preventing the chance of insulin resistance is probably the best thing you can do to make sure you live a long, healthy life.
- There are plenty of books on this subject on the market, thanks again for choosing this one! Every effort was made to ensure it is full of as much useful information as possible. Please enjoy!
- Congratulations on downloading your personal copy of *Insulin Resistance Diet Plan for Type 2*

Diabetics. Thank you for doing so.

- ## UNDERSTAND THE RESISTANCE
- There are times when our cells quit responding to our insulin. When this happens, you are likely suffering from insulin resistance. Your cells become resistant to insulin. When your body becomes resistant, your pancreas will respond by producing more insulin to try and reduce your blood sugar levels. When this happens you develop hyperinsulinemia, which is when the blood contains high levels of insulin. Let's make this a little easier, let's look at the separate parts of insulin resistance.

- **Metabolism**

- Metabolism is probably one of the most misunderstood processes that the body goes through. Your metabolism works as a collection of chemical reactions that happens in your cells to help you convert food into energy. As you are reading this, a thousand metabolic reactions are happening. There are two main metabolic channels.

- Catabolism is the process your body goes through when breaking down you food components, as in fats, proteins, and carbs, into simpler parts, which are then used for energy. To better understand it, look at it as if it is your destructive metabolism. Your cells break down fats and carbs to release their energy; this ensures that your body can fuel an anabolic reaction.

- Anabolism is the contrastive metabolism which works to build and store energy. When your cells perform an anabolic process, it helps to grow new cells and to maintain your body tissues, and it also helps to store energy that you can use later.

- The nervous and hormone systems control

these processes. When you look at how many calories you should consume in a day, you have to check your body's total energy expenditure. What you eat, how much you move, how you rest, and how well your tissues and cells recuperate will all go into figuring out your total energy expenditure.

- Your metabolism is made up of three main components:

1. Basal metabolic rate – this how many calories you body can burn while at rest, and also contributes to 50 to 80 percent of the amount of energy you body uses.

2. How much energy is used during activity – this is how many calories your body burns when you are active. This takes up 20% of your total expenditure.

3. Warming effects of your food – this is how

many calories you use when you eat, digest, and metabolize your food.

4. Insulin

5. Insulin is a hormone that the pancreas produces and releases into your blood. Insulin help to keep your blood sugar at a reasonable level by promoting cell growth and division, protein and lipid metabolism, regulating carbohydrates, and glucose uptake. Insulin helps your cells absorb glucose to use for energy.

6. After you eat, and your blood sugar levels rise, insulin is released. The glucose and insulin travel throughout your blood to your cells. It helps to stimulate the muscle tissue and liver; helps liver, fat, and muscle cells to absorb glucose; and lowers glucose levels by reducing the glucose production in your liver.

7. People who suffer from type 1 or type 2 diabetes may have to take insulin shot to help their bodies metabolize glucose correctly. Type 1 diabetic's pancreas doesn't make insulin, and the beta cells have been destroyed. There's typically no chance of preventing type 1, and most of the time a person is born with it. Type 2 diabetic's pancreas still make insulin, but the body doesn't respond to it.

8. Symptoms

9. If you go to the doctor, they will likely test your fasting insulin levels. If you have high levels, then chances are you are insulin resistant. You can also do an oral glucose tolerance test. This is where you will be given a dose of glucose, and they will check your blood sugar levels for the next few hours.

10. People who are obese or overweight, and people with a lot of fat in the mid-section, are at a greater risk of being insulin resistant. Acanthosis nigrans, a skin condition characterized by dark spots on the skin, can be a symptom of insulin resistance. Also, if you have low HDL and high triglycerides, then your chances are higher as well.

11. For the most part, insulin resistance and pre-diabetes have no significant symptoms. They main way to find out if you have either one is to get tested by your doctor. Now, you're probably wondering how to know if you should be tested. Here are some reasons why you should:

- Body Mass Index over 25
- Over age 45
- Have CVD

- Physically inactive

- Parent or sibling with diabetes

- Family background of Pacific Islander American, Hispanic/Latino, Asian American, Native American, Alaska Native, or African American

- Had a baby that weighed more than 9 pounds

- Diagnoses of gestational diabetes

- High blood pressure - 140/90 or higher

- HDL below 35 or triglyceride above 250

- Have polycystic ovary syndrome

- If your tests come back as normal, be sure to be retested every three years, at least. But, you don't have to wait until you get positive test results to start changing your life. In fact, if you have any of the risk factors, even if it's just a family history, you start changing now, and you may never have to hear that diagnoses.

- ## INSULIN RESISTANCE DIET
- Years of research has found that excess weight is the primary cause of insulin resistance. This means that weight loss can help you body better respond to insulin. Studies performed by the Diabetes Prevention Program have found that people who are pre-diabetic and insulin resistance can prevent or slow down the development of diabetes by fixing their diet.

- **Guidelines**

- Here are the main seven ways you go start to develop an insulin resistance diet:

1. Reduce Carbohydrate Intake

2. Studies that have been published in *Diabetes, Metabolic Syndrome and Obesity* suggest that controlling the number of carbohydrates you

eat is essential in controlling your glycemic index. You can count all carbs you eat, but it's best if you make sure you consume your carbs from dairy products, legumes, whole grains, fruits, and veggies.

3. Stay Away From Sweetened Beverages

4. All sugars will raise your blood sugar levels, but the American Diabetes Association has now advised, specifically, to avoid sugar-sweetened drinks. This includes iced tea, fruit drinks, soft drinks, and vitamin or energy water drinks that have artificial sweeteners, concentrates, high fructose corn syrup, or sucrose.

5. Consume More Fiber

6. Glycemia is improved in people who consume more than 50 grams of fiber each day. Large prospective cohort studies have shown that

whole grain consumption is associated with a lower risk of type 2 diabetes.

7. Consume Healthy Fats

8. Studies have shown that fatty acids are more important than total fat. People who suffer from insulin resistance should consume unsaturated fats instead of trans fatty acids or saturated fats.

9. Consume Plenty of Protein

10. *International Journal of Vitamin and Nutrition Research* published a study in 2011 that discovered people who were on a diet to treat obesity had better results when they consumed more protein.

11. Consume Dairy

12. More and more studies are finding that dairy consumption is linked to a reduced risk of type 2 diabetes.

13. Watch Your Portions

14. Losing weight is key in reducing your risk for diabetes. One great way to do that controls your portion sizes. It's best to eat more small meals instead of three large meals.

15. **Bad Foods**

16. When you start the insulin resistance diet, there are certain foods that you need to avoid, or at least reduce your intake of. Here are some of the foods that you need to watch out for.

- Red meat – contains lots of saturated fats that can exacerbate the problems
- Certain cheeses – cheese that is high in fat will cause more problems
- Fried food – this is a bad dietary choice no matter what diet you're on
- Grains – processed or refined carbs can lead

higher insulin levels

- Potatoes – these foods turn into sugar in your system

- Pumpkin – these are just like potatoes

- Carrots – these aren't entirely bad for you, just limit your intake because they are high in sugar

- Doughnuts – these are full insulin raising ingredients

- Alcohol – these turn straight to sugar when you drink them

- **Good Foods**

- Now that you know the main foods you should stay away from, here are the foods you should consume.

- Broccoli, Spinach, Collard greens – these, as well as most other leafy greens, are a great source of magnesium, zinc, vitamin E, C, and A

- Broccoli sprouts
- Swiss Chard, Romaine Lettuce, Arugula, Green Cabbage, and Kale – these also contain high amounts of nutrients
- Blueberries – contain anthocyanins which simulate the release of adiponectin which helps regular blood sugar
- Indian gooseberry – these can regulate blood sugar and reduce hyperglycemia
- Walnuts – any nut is great food for an insulin resistance diet
- These are just a few of some of the foods you should consume. Many other foods have the same properties as the ones on this list, as well as a few other types of benefits.
-
-

-
- # LONG-TERM MANAGEMENT
- Once you have started a diet, the hardest thing is sticking with it. The good thing about this diet is that it isn't anything drastic, and you can quickly change your diet with a few tweaks. To ensure that you have lasting results, let's look at some of the best ways to maintain.
- Be sure to keep up regular exercise. Exercise can help lower your blood sugar, reduce body fat, and help you lose weight. Your cells will also become more insulin sensitive as well. You don't have to do anything spectacular either. Any movement will help you; gardening, running, swimming, walking, or dancing all count for exercise.
- Remember that weight loss isn't going to be linear. You may start dropping pounds when

you first start, but you will eventually hit a plateau. You have to be proactive with your diet. When you notice you are hitting a plateau, start to make little changes to push past it.

- Try to pay attention to when you eat. If you notice that you eat when you are stress, upset, sad, bored, lonely, or low on energy take note of it. Look for other ways to move past those emotions to prevent emotional eating.
- Find some cheerleaders. I don't mean paying people to follow you around all day cheering, that would get annoying. I mean you should find a support system. The main reason why diet programs like Jenny Craig and Weight Watchers works are because of the meeting and people to talk to. There's no need to pay big bucks for this thought. You can get your family and friends to help you out, and you can

probably find a Facebook group to help you out.

- **Side Effects**
- With any diet, you will experience some side effects. These side effects will either be longer-term or short-term. Let's look at some side effects that you may experience when you begin the insulin resistance diet.
- Short-term:
    - Cravings – this is normal when you start to change your diet. Your body becomes freaked out when you start to eat healthier foods and reduce the snack foods that you're used to eating. Keep reminding yourself why you're doing this. The cravings will eventually pass.
    - Headaches – this is because your body has become addicted to the processed foods you're used to eating. You're going

to withdrawals. Once you get all the bad food out of your system, the headaches will stop.

- Lower energy - this is another symptom you will have because of withdrawals. Your energy levels will drop. Your body is doing a lot of work when you start eating healthier, so be patient with it.

- Long-term:
  - Weight loss - this is probably the best thing that will happen to you on this diet. Weight loss will help to improve all of your health problems.
  - Less hunger and cravings - you may start out having more cravings, but once that phase passes, you won't be bothered with the hunger and cravings like you used to be.

- Lower blood pressure – a diet that is low in sugar and trans and saturated fats, your blood pressure will lower. This reduces your risk of heart disease, heart attack, stroke, and several other health problems.

- More energy – getting rid of high glycemic index foods will give bursts of energy that you have never had. Plus, you will no longer have the rollercoaster effect from your blood sugar highs and lows.

- Better mood and concentration – with your old diet, you probably had mood boosts followed by a sudden plummet. With the insulin resistance diet, you will keep a more steady mood and concentration throughout the day.

- Better immune system – since you won't be consuming as many inflammatory and allergenic foods you will be able to improve your overall immune system and health.

- Increased digestion – with this diet you will reduce your intake of sugar, dairy, and gluten. These foods are the most common foods to cause digestive problems. Since you won't be consuming as many of these foods, your digestive system will work better. You will also increase your fiber intake, so this will aid your gastrointestinal tract as well.

- As you can see, the long-term side effects are better than the short-term side effects; there are also more long-term effects. It's easy to see the good outweighs the bad. It's a no brainer that this is an easy and simple diet to follow.

○

○

○

○

-
  - **DIET PLAN**
  - To help get you started, here is a 5-day meal plan. All of the recipes will follow in the next chapter.
  - <u>Day One</u>
  - Breakfast: Basil and Tomato Frittata
  - Frittatas are the perfect breakfast to help use up leftovers. Pair this with a slice of whole grain toast and fruit.
  - Lunch: Carrot and Butternut Squash Soup
  - You'll never go back to canned soups after you try this.
  - Dinner: Grilled Shrimp Skewers
  - This is a quick meal because shrimp only takes a few minutes to cook.

- Day Two
- Breakfast: Pecan, Carrot, and Banana Muffins
- This is a meal you can serve to your friends, and nobody will ever know that they are healthy. It's the perfect guilt-free treat.
- Lunch: Lemony Hummus
- Creating your hummus is a great meal. You have control over its flavor and salt levels.
- Dinner: Chicken Tortilla Soup
- This is perfect if you have some leftover chicken. This spicy soup will satisfy everyone.
- Day Three
- Breakfast: Dried Fruit, Seeds, and Nuts

Granola

- This is great to mix up a large amount on the weekend and portion it out for the following week.
- There is a high carb content because of the dried fruit, but you can easily fix that by reducing the fruit or leaving it out entirely.
- Lunch: Quinoa Tabbouleh Salad
- Quinoa is the perfect food because not only is it gluten-free, but it's also considered a protein. This is a delicious meal for meat-eaters and vegetarians.
- Dinner: Rice and Beef Stuffed Peppers
- These little peppers look sophisticated, but the entire family will love eating them up.

- <u>Day Four</u>
- Breakfast: Goat Cheese and Veggie Scramble
- This is the perfect savory breakfast. With the onions, tomatoes, peppers, eggs, and cheese you have the perfect well-rounded meal.
- Lunch: Curried Chicken Salad
- The Greek yogurt and mayo adds creaminess to the sandwich that you won't get anywhere else.
- Dinner: Jamaican Pork Tenderloin with Beans
- This is a quick summertime meal that everybody will love. Serve alongside some pilaf or brown rice.
- <u>Day Five</u>

- Breakfast: Superfood Smoothie
- This four ingredient smoothie is quick to whip up and won't run you late.
- Lunch: Tomato and Spinach Pasta
- This dish is perfect for lunch or dinner. Make a double portion so you can have some later in the week.
- Dinner: Grilled Turkey Burgers
- It should never be said that you can't have a tasty and healthy burger. Fix some sweet potato fries to complete this meal.

- RECIPES
- **Sides & Extras**
- **Salsa**
- Ingredients:
- Salt
- 1 tbsp olive oil
- ½ lime
- 1 minced garlic clove
- 1/3 c coriander, chopped
- 1 jalapeno, chopped
- 1 onion, chopped
- 2 tomatoes, chopped
- Instructions:
- Mix everything together. Add salt to your taste. Allow refrigerating for 30 minutes.

-
- **Oven-Roasted Tomatoes**
- Ingredients:
- salt
- 1 tbsp oil
- 4 thyme sprigs
- 1-pint cherry tomatoes, halved
- Instructions:
- The oven should be at 320. Place the tomatoes on a prepared baking sheet. Top with salt and thyme and drizzle with oil. Cook for 45 minutes.
-

- **Zucchini Chips**
- Ingredients:
- salt
- 1 tbsp olive oil
- 4 zucchini, sliced
- Instructions:
- Place the zucchini slices on a prepared baking sheet. Top with oil and salt.
- Cook for 30 minutes at 320 until they brown.

-

- **Breakfast**

- **Basil and Tomato Frittata**

- Ingredients:

- ½ c Italian cheese, reduced-fat

- ¼ tsp pepper

- ¼ tsp salt

- 8 egg whites

- ¼ c basil, sliced

- 2 plum tomatoes

- 1 minced garlic clove

- 2 tsp EVOO

- ¼ c onion, chopped

- Instructions:

- Cook the onion in a hot skillet until it has become tender. Mix the garlic until fragrant.

Stir in the tomato and cook until all the liquid is absorbed. Add in the basil.

- Mix the pepper, salt, and eggs. Pour into the skillet over the veggies, and top with cheese. Slide the skillet into an oven that is set to broil. Cook until the eggs are set.

-
- **Pecan, Carrot, and Banana Muffin**
- Ingredients:
- ¼ c pecans, chopped
- 1 tsp vanilla
- ½ c banana, mashed
- ¾ c carrot, shredded
- 1/3 c yogurt, sugar-free
- 1 egg
- 1/3 c brown sugar
- ¼ c canola oil
- ½ tsp salt
- ¼ tsp baking soda
- 1 tsp cinnamon
- 1 tsp baking powder
- 1 c whole wheat flour

- Instructions:

- Mix the flour, baking powder, cinnamon, baking soda, and salt together.

- Mix all the other ingredients, except for the nuts. Once combine, mix into the flour mixture. Gently fold in the pecans.

- Pour into a prepared 6-cup muffin tin. In should bake for 22 minutes at 375.

- **Homemade Granola**
- Ingredients:
- ½ c brown sugar
- 1 ½ tsp salt
- ¼ c maple syrup
- ¾ c honey
- 1 c oil
- 2 tsp vanilla
- ½ c dried apricots
- ½ c sultans
- ½ c dried cranberries
- ½ c coconut flakes
- 1 c cashews
- 1 c walnuts
- ½ c flaked almonds
- 1 c pecans, chopped
- ½ c pepitas
- 1 c sunflower seeds
- 8 c rolled oats

- Directions:
- The oven should be at 325. Mix the nuts, coconut, and oats. In a pot mix the brown sugar, vanilla, sugar, oil, honey, maple syrup and allow to boil. Let it cook for five minutes until thick. Pour the sugar mixture over the nuts and quickly stir together.
- Place the mixture on baking sheets lined with foil. Cook for 10 minutes. Remove and mix up the mixture. Bake for another 10 minutes. Once it's browned, mix in the dried fruits. Once cool, seal in a bowl or bag.
-

- **Goat Cheese and Veggie Scramble**
- Ingredients:
- ¼ c goat cheese
- ¼ tsp pepper
- ¼ tsp salt
- 1 c egg substitute
- ½ c tomato, chopped
- 2 tsp olive oil
- ¼ c onion, chopped
- ¼ c bell pepper, chopped
- Instructions:
- Cook the pepper and onion until soft. Mix in the tomato and cook until liquid is absorbed. Turn down the heat and add in the egg substitute, pepper, and salt. Scramble the egg until cooked through. Top with goat cheese.

-
- **Superfood Smoothie**
- Instructions:
- 1 banana
- 2 c spinach
- 1 c blueberries, frozen
- 1 c almond milk
- Instructions:
- Place everything in your blender and mix until smooth.

-
- **Lunch**
- **Carrot and Butternut Squash Soup**
- ¼ c half-and-half, fat-free
- ¼ tsp nutmeg
- ¼ tsp pepper
- 2 14 ½ -oz can chicken broth, reduced-sodium
- ¾ c leeks, sliced
- 2 c carrots, sliced
- 3 c butternut squash, diced
- 1 tbsp butter
- Instructions:
- Melt the butter in a large pot. Place the leek, carrot, and squash in the hot pot. Put on the lid, and allow to cook for about eight minutes. Pour in the broth. Allow everything to come to

boil. Turn down the heat to a simmer. Place the lid on the pot and let cook for 25 minutes. The veggies should be tender.

- With an immersion blender, mix the soup to the consistency that you like. Season with the nutmeg and the pepper. Bring everything back to a boil and stir in the half-and-half.

-

- **Lemony Hummus**
- Ingredients:
- ¼ c water
- 1 tbsp EVOO
- ¼ tsp cumin
- ¼ tsp pepper
- ½ tsp salt
- 1 clove garlic, chopped
- 1 ½ tbsp tahini
- ¼ c lemon juice
- 15-oz chickpeas, drained
- Directions:
- Add everything except for the water and oil in a food processor. Mix until combine. Add the oil and water and continue mixing until smooth. Add extra water if you need to.

-

- **Quinoa Tabbouleh**
- Ingredients:
- 2 scallions, sliced
- ½ c mint, chopped
- 2/3 c parsley
- 1-pint cherry tomatoes
- 1 large cucumber
- pepper
- ½ c EVOO
- 1 minced garlic clove
- 2 tbsp lemon juice
- ½ tsp salt
- 1 c quinoa, rinsed
- Instructions:
- Cook the quinoa in salted water. As the quinoa cooks, mix the garlic and lemon juice. Slowly

whisk in the EVOO, and then sprinkle with pepper and salt to your taste.

- Allow the quinoa to cool completely. Toss with the dressing and then mix in the remaining ingredients. Add extra pepper and salt if needed.

- **Curried Chicken Salad**
- Ingredients:
- 4 whole wheat pita rounds
- 2 c mixed greens
- 1 c green grapes
- ¼ tsp pepper
- ¼ tsp salt
- 1 tsp curry powder
- 3 tbsp mayo, reduced-fat
- ½ c Greek yogurt, nonfat
- ¼ c slivered almonds
- 1 ¼-lb chicken, shredded
- Instructions:
- Mix all of the ingredients except for the greens and pitas. Divide the chicken mixture into each pita. Top each with some greens.

-

- **Tomato and Spinach Pasta**
- Instructions:
- 3 tbsp parmesan, grated
- 1 tbsp balsamic vinegar
- ¼ tsp pepper
- 2 minced garlic cloves
- 1 c grape tomatoes
- 8 c spinach
- 2 tbsp olive oil
- 8-oz whole-wheat spaghetti
- Instructions:
- Cook the spaghetti the way the package says to, but without the salt. Drain.
- As the pasta cooks, sauté the spinach until it wilts. Stir in the tomatoes and cook for about three minutes. Mix in the garlic.

- Toss the pasta with the veggies and all the other ingredients.

-
- **Dinner**

- **Grilled Shrimp Skewers**

- Ingredients:

- 9 skewers, soaked

- 1 lb cleaned shrimp

- 2 scallions, minced

- ¼ tsp pepper

- ½ tsp salt

- ¼ tsp red pepper flakes

- 1 medium lemon, zest, and juice

- 2 minced garlic cloves

- 1 ½ tbsp olive oil

- Instructions:

- Prepare your grill.

- Mix the scallions, pepper, salt, pepper flakes,

lemon juice and zest, garlic, and oil.

- Place the shrimp in the mixture and coat. Allow to marinate in the refrigerate for 30 minutes.

- Place the shrimp evenly among the skewers. Get rid on any remaining marinade.

- Grill them shrimp until pink and firm, around two to three minutes.

-

- **Chicken Tortilla Soup**
- Ingredients:
- 1 c tortilla chips
- 2 minced garlic cloves
- 1 c chicken broth, reduced-sodium
- 2 c stir-fry veggies
- 2 c chicken, shredded
- 2 ½ c water
- 1 14 ½-oz can stewed tomatoes, Mexican-style
- Directions:
- In a crock pot, mix the garlic, broth, veggies, chicken, water, and tomatoes.
- Cook for six and a half hours on low.
- Top with chips.

-
- **Rice and Beef Stuffed Peppers**
- Ingredients:
- 1 tbsp parsley, divided
- ½ tsp pepper
- 2 tsp salt
- 4 minced garlic cloves
- ½ c tomato sauce
- ¼ c parsley
- ½ c Parmigiano-Reggiano, shredded
- 1 ½ c rice, cooked
- 1 ½ lb ground beef
- ¼ tsp red pepper flakes
- 1 c beef broth
- ½ onion, sliced
- 2 ½ c tomato sauce
- 6 bell peppers
- Instructions:
- The oven should be at 375. Cut the tops off the peppers and clean out the insides. Poke a few

small holes in the bottom of each.

- Place 2 ½ cups tomato sauce in a casserole dish. Place in the pepper flakes, broth, and onion. Set the peppers upright in the mixture.
- Mix the pepper, salt, garlic, 2 tbsp tomato sauce, ¼ c parsley, cheese, rice, and beef. Divide the mixture between the peppers. Add a tablespoon of tomato sauce on top of each and lay the pepper tops back on. Top dish with parchment paper and then tin foil. Place the dish on a baking sheet.
- Cook for an hour. They should be starting to feel soft. Take off the foil and parchment and cook for an addition 25 minutes.
-

- **Jamaican Pork Tenderloin**
- Ingredients:
- ½ tsp pepper
- ¼ tsp salt
- 1 tbsp lemon juice
- 1 tsp lemon zest
- 1 tbsp EVOO
- 1 lb green beans
- 3 c water
- 2 tbsp Creole mustard
- ¼ c grape jelly
- 2 tsp Jerk seasoning
- ¼ c orange juice, divided
- ¾ lb pork tenderloin
- Instructions:
- Mix the pepper, salt, lemon juice and zest, EVOO and water. Bring everything to a boil and add in the beans.
- As the beans cook, mix the mustard, jelly, jerk

seasoning, and half the orange juice. Cover the tenderloin. The oven should be set and 350. Place the tenderloin in a casserole dish and pour in the rest of the orange juice. Bake for 45 minutes.

-

- **Grilled Turkey Burgers**
- Ingredients:
- 4 whole-wheat buns
- ½ tsp curry
- ¼ c Dijon
- 12-oz ground turkey
- 1/8 tsp pepper
- ¼ tsp garlic salt
- ¼ tsp Italian seasoning
- 2 tbsp milk, fat-free
- 2 tbsp bread crumbs
- ¼ c green onions, sliced
- ½ c carrot, shredded
- Instructions:
- Mix the ground turkey with the seasonings, bread crumbs, and veggies. Form the meat mixture into four patties.
- Prepare your grill, and cook the patties until done.

- Mix the mustard and curry powder and spread onto the buns. Add the burgers to the buns. Top with tomato and lettuce if desired.

-

- **Dessert**

- **Blueberries and Yogurt**

- Ingredients:

- 1/3 c Greek yogurt

- 10 blueberries

- Instructions:

- Top the yogurt with the blueberries and enjoy.

-

-
- **Raspberry Sorbet**
- Ingredients:
- lemon juice
- 1 c raspberries
- Instructions:
- Place the ingredients in a food processor and mix until smooth. Place in an airtight container and freeze.
-

-
-
-
-

BOOK THREE

CROCK POT

MASTERY COOKBOOK

The Zero Effort Crock Pot Recipes For Everyone

DIANA WATSON

-
-
-
-
-
-
-
-
-
-
-
-
- **Table of Contents**

- Introduction

- [Chapter 1: The Power of the Crock Pot and Its Benefits](#)
- [Chapter 2: Healthy Breakfast Recipes](#)
- [Chapter 3: Time-Saving Lunch Specialties](#)
- [Chapter 4: Dinner in a Hurry](#)
- [Chapter 5: Desserts - Snacks and Treats to Devour](#)
- [Chapter 6: Index for the Recipes](#)C
- [Conclusion](#)
-
-
-
-
- **VIP Subscriber List**

- Hi Dear Reader, this is Diana! If you like my book and you want to receive the latest tips and tricks on cooking, weight-loss, cookbook recipes and more, do subscribe to my mailing list in the link here! I will then be able to send you the most up-to-date information about my upcoming books and promotions as well! Thank you for supporting my work and happy reading!
-
-

-
- © Copyright 2017 by Diana Watson - All rights reserved.
- The following eBook is reproduced below with the goal of providing information that is as accurate and as reliable as possible. Regardless, purchasing this eBook can be seen as consent to the fact that both the publisher and the author of this book are in no way experts on the topics discussed within, and that any recommendations or suggestions made herein are for entertainment purposes only. Professionals should be consulted as needed before undertaking any of the action endorsed herein.
- This declaration is deemed fair and valid by both the American Bar Association and the Committee of Publishers Association and is legally binding throughout the United States.
- Furthermore, the transmission, duplication or reproduction of any of the following work, including precise information, will be considered an illegal act, irrespective whether it is done electronically or in print. The legality extends to creating a secondary or tertiary copy of the work or a recorded copy and is only allowed with express written consent of the Publisher. All additional rights are reserved.
- The information in the following pages is broadly considered to be a truthful and accurate account of facts, and as such any inattention, use or misuse of the information in question by the reader will render any resulting actions solely under their purview. There are no scenarios in which the publisher or the original author of this work can be in any fashion deemed liable for any hardship or

damages that may befall them after undertaking information described herein.
- Additionally, the information found on the following pages is intended for informational purposes only and should thus be considered, universal. As befitting its nature, the information presented is without assurance regarding its continued validity or interim quality. Trademarks that mentioned are done without written consent and can in no way be considered an endorsement from the trademark holder.
-
-
-
-
-
-
-
-
-
-
-
-
-
-
-
-
-
-
-
-
-
-
-
-
-
-

-
- **Introduction**
- Congratulations on purchasing your personal copy of *Crock Pot Mastery Cookbook: The Zero Effort Crock Pot Recipe Guide For Everyone.* Thank you for doing so. You will quickly determine how you can come home and relax because you know your meal will be waiting for you in the kitchen!
- You might not realize how versatile your Crock Pot is, but its capability to be a slow cooker is only the beginning as you will soon discover. You will enjoy making tasty, and less time-consuming meals that you and your family will enjoy. From frugal to fancy; the recipe is here for the taking.
- You will discover how important using your pot can be. It will give you all of the added time that you can spend with your family and friends since you don't have to slave over the oven to provide a nutritious meal for yourself and them.
- For some of the recipes; you will notice distinct sizes mentioned for the Crock-Pot®. These unit sizes are provided because they are the best sizes tested for the exact times suggested for each of the recipes whether it is lunch, dinner, or breakfast meals. You may need to make some minor adjustments, but it will be a quick fix.
- The following chapters will discuss some of the many different ways you can benefit from using the Crock-Pot®, not only with the time saved but many health benefits as well.
- There is an abundance of books on this subject on the market, thanks again for choosing this one! Every effort was made to ensure it is full

of as much useful information as possible. Please enjoy!

-
-
-
-

-
- Chapter 1: The Power of the Crock Pot and Its Benefits
- **The Ways You Can Benefit**
- Think of how many times you have experienced 'spells' that you did not feel like spending hours over the stove preparing dinner. Can you relate? How about the times during the holidays when you are planning on a houseful of guests; yikes? By the way, "Don't sweat it because you have your fabulous cooker and all of these new recipes to try out."
- These are a few ways to make the path a bit easier:
- *Get Ahead of the Meal:* Preparing food with your Crock-Pot® can put you ahead of the game the night before you have a busy day planned. You can always make the meal for the next day in just a few minutes. Put all of the ingredients (if they can combine overnight) into the pot, so when you get up the next morning; all you need to do is take it out of the fridge, and let it get to room temperature. Turn it on as you head out of the door and dinner will be ready when you get home. YES!
- *Save a lot of Effort and Time:* All it takes is a few good recipes and a little bit of your valuable time. In most of the cases, these recipes are geared towards a fast lifestyle and will be ready with just a few simple steps. After some time and practice, you will know exactly which ones will be your favorites; all of them!
- *Cut Back on Dining Out:* Having an enjoyable meal at home is so much more personal for your family because you (and your pot) prepared it! Not only that, You will eliminate the temptation to order foods that might not

be so healthy and in turn—will be more expensive.
- *Watching the Extra Liquids*: There is no need to use additional ingredients, other than what is described within each of the recipes. Ideally, you should not fill the more than half to two-thirds full of ingredients. Too much liquid will cause a leakage from the top and may result in improperly cooked food.
- *Cook it Slow & Leave it Alone:* A slow cooker is known for creating delicious dishes while bringing out all of the natural flavors. So, go ahead and go to work or have some fun—or—better yet go to bed early! There is no need to worry about checking on it (unless the recipe calls for it). Each time the lid is removed—valuable heat is escaping—resulting in a breakdown of the advised times. Just keep that element it in mind, even though it smells so good!
- *Trimming the Fat*: One huge advantage to the use of this type of cooking is you can save quite a chunk of money purchasing cheaper cuts of meat. Also, capitalize on the flavorful meat in small quantities and by bulking up on veggies with smaller meat portions.
- **Hot Antioxidants**
- Many recent studies have discovered cooking some food items such as tomatoes will increase the bioavailability of many of the nutrients. For example, lycopene which is linked to cancer and heart prevention becomes move available to the body because the heat releases the lycopene.
- A study from 2003 compared the content of fresh, frozen, and canned corn which was processed with heat; specifically lutein and xeaxanthin, and found less lutein in the fresh

version. This lutein is mostly well-known to protect you from some eye diseases.
- Score 'ONE' for the Crock-Pot®.
- *Who Knew?*
- **Basic Times & Settings**
- The question always arises of how long you should cook your items if you don't have a recipe for a Crock-Pot®. These are only general guidelines because the size of a pot will make a difference in the cooking times.

Regular Cooking Times	Crock Pot® High Temperatures	Crock Pot® Low Pot Temperatures
Hours		
1/4 to 1/2	1 to 2	4 to 6
1/2 to 1	2 to 3	5 to 7
1 to 2	3 to 4	6 to 8
2 to 4	4 to 6	8 to 12

-
- *Note:* You must consider that root veggies take longer than other vegetables and meats which mean they should be placed in the lower part of the pot.
- Are You Ready? Of course, you are!
-
-
-
-
-
- Chapter 2: Healthy Breakfast Recipes
- Boiled Eggs
- Did you ever wake up in the middle of the night for a 'potty' break, and decided you want some boiled eggs or egg salad for breakfast or

work tomorrow, but do not have the time to sit around and wait for the eggs to cook? You have a cure for that!
- *Ingredients and Instructions*
- The simplicity is amazing!
1) Pour some water into the Crock-Pot®, add as many eggs as you want, and set the pot for 3 ½ hours on the low setting. Go back to bed and enjoy tomorrow!

2) One-Hour Bread
3) Crave that fresh bread—no longer! You can have some delicious comfort food shortly!
4) Ingredients
5) 1 ½ C. Baking Mix
6) 3 Tbsp. Italian Seasoning
7) ½ cup milk (skim is okay)
8) *Optional:* ½ C. shredded cheese or 3 Tbsp. Grated Parmesan cheese
9) Directions
1) Prepare the cooker with some non-stick cooking spray.

2) Combine all of the ingredients until the lumps are gone and empty into the cooker.

3) *Notes:* Bisquick® is a good choice.

4) Breakfast Fiesta Delight
5) Directions

6) 1 Pound Country-Style Sausage
7) 1 Package (28-ounces) frozen hash brown potatoes (thawed)
8) ½ Cup whole milk
9) 12 large eggs
10) 1 ½ Cups shredded Mexican blend cheese

11) Directions

1) Prepare the Crock-Pot® by spraying it with some cooking spray to help with the cleanup.

2) Brown and crumble the sausage in a frying pan; remove and pat the grease away using a paper towel.

3) Whip the eggs together in a mixing container.

4) Layer the ingredients with a layer of potatoes, cheese, sausage, and eggs.

5) *Serving Time*: Have some salsa, sour cream, pepper, and salt for a tasty topping.

6) *Servings*: Six to Eight
7) *Prep Time* is fifteen minutes
8) *Cooking Time* is six to eight hours.

9) Italian Sausage Scramble

10) Ingredients

11) 1 ½ Lbs. Italian sausage
12) 1 medium yellow onion

13) 6 medium red potatoes
14) ¼ Cup fresh Italian minced parsley
15) One medium diced tomato
16) 1 Cup frozen/fresh kernel corn
17) 2 cups grated Cheddar cheese
18) Directions
1) Discard the outer casing from the sausage.

   Peel and dice the onions and potatoes.

2) Sauté the onion and crumbled sausage until browned. Place them on a few paper towels to absorb the grease/fat and add the items to the slow cooker.

3) Combine the rest of the ingredients—blending well. Cover and cook.

4) *Servings*: Six
5) *Prep Time* is 15 Minutes.
6) *Cook Time:* The high setting is for four hours, and the lower setting is for six to eight hours.
7)
8)
9) The Sweeter Side of Breakfast
10) Blueberry Steel Cut Oats
11) Ingredients
12) 1 ½ C. of water
13) 2 C. frozen blueberries
14) 1 banana
15) 1 C. Steel cut oats
16) 1- ½ C. Vanilla almond milk

17) 1 Tbsp. butter
18) 1 ½ tsp. cinnamon
19) *Directions*
1) Prepare a six-quart cooker with the butter, making sure to cover the sides also.

2) Mash the banana slightly and add all of the ingredients into the Pot—stirring gently.

3) Place the top on the crock pot and cook for *one hour* on the HIGH setting; switch to the WARM setting overnight, and sleep tight!

4) Wake up ready for a busy day by adding a drizzle of honey and get moving!
5) *Servings*: Four to Six
6) *Preparation Time*: Fifteen Minutes
7) *Cooking Time*: Eight hours
8) Pumpkin Pie Oatmeal
9) *Ingredients*
10) 1 C. oats (steel cut)
11) 3 ½ C. water
12) 1 C. pumpkin puree
13) ¼ tsp. each:
- salt

- vanilla extract

- pumpkin pie spices

- *Optional:* 2 Tbsp. maple syrup
- *Directions*

1) Use some non-stick cooking spray to coat the Crock-Pot®.

2) Empty the oats into the Pot.

3) Mix the remainder of the ingredients in a large mixing container, and pour over the oats.

4) *Note*: If you like sweeter oatmeal just adjust the flavor after it is cooked.

5) *Cooking Time*: Eight hours on low
6) **Pumpkin Butter**
7) *Ingredients*
8) 4 Cups pumpkin
9) 1 tsp. ground ginger
10) 2 tsp. cinnamon
11) 1-¼ Cups honey/maple syrup
12) ½ tsp. nutmeg
13) 1 tsp. vanilla extract (*optional*)
14) *Instructions*

1) Blend the vanilla, syrup/honey, and pumpkin puree in the Crock-Pot®.

2) Cover and cook. During the last hour—add the ginger, cinnamon, and nutmeg.

3) If you want it a little thicker, you can crack the lid. After all, the aroma is tantalizing—especially first thing in the morning!

4) You can store in jars in the bottom of the fridge for a healthy addition—anytime.
5) *Yields:* About 10 ounces
6) *Preparation Time*: Five Minutes
7) *Cooking Time*: Five hours

8)
9)
10) Chapter 3: Time-Saving Lunch Specialties
11) Beef Tacos
12) Ingredients
13) 1 Package taco seasoning
14) 1 (ten-ounce) Can tomatoes and green chilies (Rotel)
15) 1 Pound lean ground beef
16) Directions
1) Add everything listed into your Crock-Pot®.

2) If you are available; stir every couple of hours to break up the beef or break it up before serving.

3) Serve on a floured tortilla or taco shell with your choice of toppings.

4) *Servings*: 12 tacos
5) *Preparation Time*: Two Minutes
6) *Cooking Time*: Five to Six Hours
7) Root Beer & BBQ Chicken
8) Ingredients
9) 1 (18-ounce) bottle barbecue sauce
10) 4 chicken breasts
11) ¼ teaspoon each pepper and salt
12) ½ can or bottle root beer (full-sugar)
13) *Note:* You can use Dr. Pepper or Coke instead of root beer.
14) Directions

1) Pour the drink of choice, and place the chicken in the cooker.

2) Drain once the chicken has finished cooking, and discard most of the liquid—but leaving enough to prevent dryness.

3) Flavor with some pepper and salt if desired and empty the contents of the sauce into the Crock-Pot®, cooking for about 15 to 20 minutes.

4) Enjoy on some burger buns or rolls.

5) *Cooking Time*: The high temperature will have it ready in 3 hours.
6) Stuffed Banana Peppers
7) Ingredients
8) 1 Package Italian Sausage
9) Banana Peppers
10) 2 Jars of Marinara Sauce (approximately)
11) Directions
1) Adapt this for your crowd on the amounts used.

2) Remove both ends of the peppers and scoop

out the seeds and discard them.

3) Pour ½ of the jar of sauce in the Crock-Pot®.

4) Dice the sausage, in case it is not already prepared.

5) Stuff the pepper with the sausage and put them into the Pot.

6) Pour the sauce over the banana peppers.

7) *Cooking Time*: Low for eight to nine hours
8) Crock-Pot® Taco Soup
9) *Ingredients*
10) 1 (14.5-ounces) Can Each:
- Beef broth

- Petite diced tomatoes

- 1 (15-ounces) Can Each:
- Black beans

- Corn

- 1 (10-ounces) Can Rotel Original
- 1 Can kidney beans (16-ounces)
- 1 (1-oz.) pouch each:
- Taco seasoning mix

- Ranch seasoning mix (Hidden Valley)

- ½ teaspoon salt
- 1 ½ teaspoons onion powder
- 1 Lb. ground beef
- *Garnish*: Sour Cream, Fritos, chopped green onions, or some shredded cheddar cheese
- *Notes:* The recipe is excellent if you choose the 'Diced Tomatoes with Green Chilies.'
- *Directions*

1) Cook the beef and drain. Rinse and drain all of the cans of veggies except for the chilies; reserve the liquid from the corn and tomatoes.

2) Toss everything into the Crock-Pot® (except for the garnishes).

3) Cook for the necessary time.

4) When the process is completed, add the garnishes of your choice with some Fritos on the side to complement the flavors

5) *Servings*: 8 to 10
6) *Prep Time*: Ten minutes
7) *Cook Time*: Low for 4 hrs. or High for 2 hrs.
8)
9)
10)

11)
12)
13)

14)
15)
16) Chapter 4: Dinner in a Hurry
17) Beef
18) Meat for the Tacos
19) Ingredients
20) 2 Lbs. Ground beef (lean)
21) 1 cup diced onions/Birds Eye Chopped Onions and Garlic
22) 1 Package low-sodium taco seasoning mix
23) Directions
1) Put the burger into the Crock-Pot® and cook it for four to six hours. If you are in the area of the kitchen—stir the meat every couple of hours to ensure it is cooking evenly (if not—no worries).

2) When the cooking cycle is complete; drain the beef on some paper towels.

3) Combine the onions and ½ to one package of the taco seasoning.

4) Blend well and continue cooking for about one more hour

5) *Servings*: Six
6) *Preparation Time*: Five Minutes
7) *Cooking Time*: Low setting: Four to Six hours
8) Steak Pizzaiola
9) Ingredients
10) 1 (one to two pounds) London Broil
11) 1 Yellow, orange, or red sliced bell pepper
12) 1 Large sliced onion
13) ¼ Cup water
14) ½ to ¾ of a jar (your choice) tomato pasta sauce
15) Directions
1) Flavor the meat with the pepper and salt and place it into the Crock-Pot®.

2) Add the peppers and onions, followed by your favorite sauce,

3) Cook for six to eight hours. (Flip a time or two if you are home.)

4) Serve over some pasta, potatoes, or veggies.

5) *Cooking Time*: Low heat for six to eight hours
6) Steaks in the Pot
7) Ingredients
8) 4 to 6 steaks
9) ¼ C. White Wine
10) 2 T. A-1 Sauce
11) 2 T. Dijon mustard
12) Directions
1) Blend the mustard and steak sauce; add it to

each of the pieces of steak.

2) Add the meat into the Crock-Pot®, add the wine, and cook for six to eight hours.

3) *Servings*: Four or More
4) *Cooking Time*: 6 to 8 Hours on the low setting
5) Chicken and Turkey
6) Buffalo Chicken
7) *Ingredients*
8) 3 to 5 Pounds (no skin or bones) chicken breasts
9) 1 (12-ounce) Bottle Red Hot Wings Buffalo Sauce
10) 1 Pouch ranch dressing mix
11) *Directions*
1) Put the chicken into the Crock-Pot®. Empty the sauce over the breasts and sprinkle the ranch mix over the top. Cover and Cook.

2) Take the chicken out of the Pot and throw away the sauce.

3) Shred the chicken with a couple of forks. It should be tender.

4) Put it back into the cooker and stir to coat the chicken thoroughly.

5) Leave it in the pot on low about one more hour. Most of the sauce will be absorbed.

6) *Cooking Time*: Low for five hours
7) Caesar Chicken
8) Ingredients
9) 1 bottle (12-ounces) Caesar dressing
10) 4 skinless & boneless chicken breasts
11) ½ Cup shredded Parmesan cheese
12) Directions
1) Add the breasts of chicken to the Crock-Pot®.

2) Cook the chicken for the specified time and drain the juices.

3) Empty the dressing over the breasts.

4) Sprinkle the cheese on top of that and cook for thirty more minutes covered until done.

5) Have a side of Caesar salad to complement the meal.
6) *Servings*: Four
7) *Prep Time*: 5 minutes
8) *Cooking Time*: Use the low setting for 6 hrs. ; the high setting High for 3 hrs.
9) Cranberry Chicken
10) Ingredients
11) 4 (no skin or bones) Chicken Breasts
12) 1 (8-ounces) bottle Kraft Catalina dressing
13) 1 Pouch dry onion soup

14) 1 (14-ounces) Can Ocean Spray Whole Cranberry Sauce

15) Directions

1) Cook the chicken in the Crock-Pot® according to your specified times. Drain the juices.

2) Combine the cranberry sauce, onion soup mix, and dressing. Empty it over the chicken.

3) Cook—covered—about 30 minutes.

4) *Servings*: Four
5) *Preparation Time*: Five minutes
6) *Cooking Time*: High for three hours or low for six hours

7) French Onion Chicken

8) Ingredients

9) 4 Chicken breasts (no bones or skin)
10) 1 Can French Onion soup (10.5-ounces)
11) ½ cup sour cream

12) Directions

1) Put the breasts in the Pot and cook for the stated time. Empty the liquids.

2) Combine the soup and sour cream and add into the pot on top of the chicken

3) breasts.
4) Cook covered for about 30 minutes.

5) *Servings*: Four
6) *Preparation Time*: Five Minutes
7) *Cooking Time*: The high setting will take approximately three hours, whereas the low setting takes six hours.

8) Hawaiian Chicken

9) Ingredients
10) 4 to 5 skinless and boneless breasts of chicken (thawed)
11) 1 (20-oz.) Can Dole Pineapple Chunks
12) 1 Bottle (12-oz.) Heinz Chili Sauce
13) 1/3 C. brown sugar

14) Directions
1) Cook the chicken until its predetermined time limit is completed. Empty the liquid.

2) Combine the brown sugar, ½ of the juices of the can of pineapples, the chili sauce, and the chunks of pineapple.

3) Empty the mixture over the drained breasts and heat on the high setting for approximately 30 minutes or so.

4) Have a bit of pineapple in every bite. Yummy!

5) *Servings*: 4 to 5
6) *Preparation Time*: 5 min.
7) *Cooking Time*: High = 6 hrs. / Low = 3 hrs.

8) Honey Mustard Chicken

9) Ingredients
10) 1 (12-ounces) Bottle Dijon mustard
11) 1/3 C. honey
12) 4 skinless & boneless chicken breasts (thawed)
13) Directions
1) Cook the chicken for its predetermined time and dispose of the juices.

2) Combine the mustard and honey in a small dish.

3) Empty the sauce over the chicken and cook for about ½ hour (covered) until done,

4) *Servings*: Four
5) *Preparation Time*: Five Minutes
6) *Cooking Time*: Use the low setting for six hrs. Or on high for three hrs.
7) Chicken Italian Style
8) Ingredients
9) 4 chicken breasts (thawed – no bones- no skin)
10) 1 (16-ounce) Bottle Italian Dressing
11) Directions
1) Place the breasts of chicken into your Crock-Pot® and pour the dressing on them.

2) Put the lid on and let it do your work!

3) *Servings*: Four

4) *Preparation Time*: 5 minutes
5) *Cooking Time*: Use the high setting to prepare the chicken for 3.5 hrs. Or use the low setting for 7 hours.
6) Swedish Meatballs
7) *Ingredients*
8) 1 (12-ounce) jar Heinz HomeStyle Gravy (Savory Beef)
9) 1 (eight-ounce) container of sour cream
10) 1 Bag Frozen Meatballs
11) *Instructions*
1) Empty the gravy into the Crock-Pot®, followed by the sour cream.

2) Combine these until they are completely blended.

3) Toss the package of frozen meatballs into the Pot filling to approximately 2/3 to ¾ of the space.

4) Place the lid on the pot and cook—occasionally stirring if you happen to be close to the kitchen.

5) You can always make more or less of the recipe depending on how many people you will

serve.

6) *Cooking Time*: Low for a minimum of 5 hours
7) **Sweet and Sour Chicken**
8) *Ingredients*
9) 1 (22-ounces) Bag frozen Tyson Chicken Breast
10) 2 Cups cooked rice/steamed vegetables (or both)
11) 1 bottle (18-ounces) Apricot Preserves
12) 1 jar (12-ounces) chili sauce
13) *Directions*
1) Layer the frozen chicken pieces into the Crock-Pot®.

2) Combine the preserves and chili sauce in a small container (a mixing cup is ideal). Empty it over the chicken. *Note:* You can also use pineapple or a combination.

3) Toss to mix and let the Pot do the work.

4) Enjoy with some veggies and rice.

5) *Servings*: Six (one cup per serving)
6) *Cooking Time* on the high setting is 2 to 3 hours.
7) **Creamy Taco Chicken**
8) *Ingredients*
9) 1 Can Rotel Original Tomatoes with Green

Chilies
10) 3 chicken breasts (no bone or skin)
11) 4-ounces cream cheese (regular or light)

12) Directions
1) Pour the tomatoes, and place the chicken into the slow cooker.

2) A few minutes before the end of the cooking cycle, use a fork or tongs to shred the chicken.

3) Put the cream cheese on top of the mixture, but don't stir.

4) By the time the meal is ready, the cheese will be oozing into your chicken. Yummy!

5) *Suggestions*: You can use this in a casserole, over rice, as a salad, or any other creative plan you may have for your meal.
6) *Cooking Time*: Low temperature - Six to Eight hours

7) Stuffed – Roasted Turkey

8) Ingredients
9) 2 C. Stuffing Mix
10) Black pepper and salt
11) 6 Pounds Turkey
12) 1 Tablespoon melted butter

13) Instructions
1) Use the package instructions to prepare the stuffing.

2) Flavor the turkey with some melted butter, pepper, and salt.

3) Prepare the bird by loosely placing the stuffing in the carcass.

4) Cover and let the Pot do the rest.

5) *Servings*: Four
6) *Cooking Time*: Low: 9 to 11 hours; High: 5 hours

7) Fish
8) Citrus Flavored Fish

9) Ingredients
10) Pepper and Salt
11) 1 ½ pounds fish fillets
12) 1 medium chopped onion
13) 4 tsp. oil
14) 5 Tbsp. Chopped parsley
15) 2 tsp. Each grated: lemon and orange rind
16) *Garnish*: Lemon and orange slices
17) Directions
18) Use some butter to grease the Crock-Pot®.
1) Flavor the fish with some pepper and salt and put it into the pot.

2) Add the parsley, grated rinds, and onion as well as the oil over the fish.

3) Cover and cook.

4) When ready to eat; garnish with some lemon

or orange slices.

5) *Cooking Time*: 1 ½ Hours on Low
6) Salmon Bake
7) Ingredients
8) 3 (one-pound) Cans Salmon
9) 1 (16-ounces) can tomato puree
10) 4 cups bread crumbs (10 slices worth)
11) 1 chopped green pepper
12) 3 teaspoons lemon juice
13) 2 crushed chicken bouillon cubes
14) 1 Can each (condensed) cream of onion soup & cream of celery soup
15) 6 (well-beaten) eggs
16) ½ cup milk
17) Directions
1) Use some cooking spray or other oil to grease the Crock-Pot® lightly.

2) Blend all of the ingredients—except for the milk and celery soup into the Pot.

3) Cover and cook.

4) Combine and stir the milk and celery soup in a small pan to use as a sauce for the salmon.

5) When the salmon is done, garnish and enjoy with the special sauce!

6) *Cooking Time*: High for three hours or low for four to six hours
7) Pork
8) BBQ Style Pork Steaks
9) Ingredients
10) 4 (½-inch cut) Pork shoulder steaks
11) 2 large sliced tomatoes
12) 1 large onion
13) 1 large thinly sliced bell pepper
14) 1 Tbsp. Each:
- Vegetable oil

- Tapioca (quick-cooking)

- ¼ C. red wine
- ½ tsp. cumin
- ½ C. barbecue sauce (your choice)
- *Directions*

1) Slice and cut the onion as if you are preparing to make onion rings for dinner.

2) Trim away an excess fat and slice the steaks in half - lengthwise.

3) Brown the steaks in skillet using hot oil, and drain on paper towels.

4) Organize the peppers, tomatoes, and onions in the Crock-Pot®; sprinkling the tapioca over

them. Place the pork in last.

5) Prepare the cumin, wine, and barbecue sauce in a small dish. Pour it over the ingredients in the Pot, and cover.

6) *Servings*: Four
7) *Cooking Time*: Low Heat – Six to Eight Hours (or until veggies and meat are tender)
8) *Note*: The recipe is based on a 3 ½- or a 4-quart Crock-Pot®. If you have a different size the cooking time may vary.

9) Pepsi® Roast

10) Ingredients
11) 1 Can Cream of mushroom soup
12) 5 Lb. Pork Roast/ Steak/Chops
13) ½ package dry onion soup mix
14) 1 can Regular Pepsi (Don't use Diet)

15) Directions

1) Put the meat in the Crock-Pot® first and sprinkle with the soup mix.

2) Empty the mushroom soup and Pepsi over the meat.

3) Close the lid and let the pot do the rest of the chore.

4) *Suggestion*: Use the sauce to pour over some

rice or potatoes.
5) *Servings*: Eight
6) *Cooking Time*: Low setting for six to seven hours

7) Ranch Chops

8) Ingredients
9) Pouch – Ranch Dressing Mix
10) Pork Chops
11) 1 Can Cream of Chicken Soup Plus (+) 1 Can Water OR 2 Cups Cream of Chicken

12) Directions
1) Pour the liquids into the Crock-Pot® along with the chops and dressing mix.

2) *Cooking Time*: Use the low-temperature setting for four to six hours.

3) Ham in Cider Gravy
4) This ham is so tasty it cannot remain in the 'breakfast only' slot. It is so tasty and can advance to lunch and dinner menus as well.

5) Ingredients
6) 1 (one to four pound) Ham
7) ¾ cup maple syrup
8) 2 cups unsweetened apple cider
9) 3 Tablespoons cornstarch

10) Directions
1) Arrange the ham in the Crock-Pot® and top it off with the syrup and cider.

2) Cook until the time indicated below is completed.

3) Move the ham to a serving platter. Pour the

liquid into a large cup (a measuring cup is perfect).

4) Whisk ½ of the cider and the cornstarch on the stovetop using the low-temperature setting until it is smooth. Continue whisking and increase the burner to med-low—adding small amounts of cider at a time—until the gravy is bubbly and thickened to the desired consistency.

5) *Servings*: Four to Eight
6) *Preparation Time*: Four minutes
7) *Cooking Time*: Low - six to eight hours
8) Casseroles
9) Crock-Pot® Dinner: Beef or Chicken
10) *Ingredients*
11) 1 Whole/cut up chicken –or– legs and thighs OR a Beef Roast
12) 2 Carrots
13) 4 Potatoes
14) 5 Ounces water
15) 1 Can celery or cream of mushroom soup (10 ¾ ounce)
16) *Directions*
1) Cut the carrots into four-inch chunks. Put all of the ingredients into the Crock-Pot®.

2) Set the Pot and let it 'go.'

3) *Servings*: Four
4) *Cooking Time*: The high setting will cook the meal in six hours, or you can cook it all day using the low-temperature setting.
5) **Squash 'N Chops**
6) *Ingredients*
7) 5 Pork (boneless) Port cutlets or chops
8) 2 medium oranges
9) 1 ¼ Pounds delicate/butternut squash
10) 1/8 tsp. Ground red pepper
11) ½ tsp. Garlic salt
12) ¼ tsp. Each: Ginger, cloves, and cinnamon
13) *Directions*
1) Peel and slice the oranges. Peel and slice the squash lengthwise and discard the seeds. Cut the 'half' into sections ½-inches thick.

2) Flavor the pork with some garlic salt and red peppers. Use a 4- to 5- quart Crock-Pot® and place the chops/cutlets in the bottom.

3) Combine the ginger, cinnamon, and cloves in a small dish.

4) Top off the pork with the oranges along with the toppings in step 3.

5) Cover and cook.

6) *Servings*: 5
7) *Cooking Time*: Low for 4 hours
8) Lasagna Enchantment
9) This one has a few more steps, but it is so worth it—and it's easy.
10) Ingredients
11) 2 Cans diced tomatoes (28-ounces) drained
12) Four finely chopped clove of garlic
13) 2 Tbsp. oregano
14) ½ tsp. salt
15) 15-ounces fresh ricotta
16) ¼ tsp. pepper
17) ½ tsp. salt
18) ½ C. shredded Parmesan cheese
19) 1 (12-ounce) Package uncooked lasagna noodles
20) ½ tsp. fresh (finely chopped) parsley – more if desired
21) 2 C. spinach leaves (bagged is okay)
22) 2 C. shredded Mozzarella cheese
23) Directions
1) Mix the garlic, drained tomatoes, pepper, salt, and oregano in a mixing container.

2) In another bowl, blend the parsley, Parmesan, and ricotta cheese.

3) Dip anywhere from 1/3 to ½ cup of the tomato combination on the base of the Crock-Pot®.

4) Layer the noodles, spinach, several dollops of the ricotta combo, and 1/3 to about ½ of the tomato combination. Sprinkle the mozzarella on the top of that section. Continue the process with the mozzarella on the top.

5) Close the lid on the Pot and let it do the work.

6) *Servings*: Six to Eight
7) *Prep Time*: 20 Minutes
8) *Cook Time*: High is 2 Hrs. or Low is 3 to 4 Hrs.
9) Sweet Potato Casserole
10) Ingredients
11) 1 ½ C. applesauce
12) 1 tsp. ground cinnamon
13) 3 Tbsp. Margarine/butter
14) ½ C. Toasted chopped nuts
15) 2/3 C. Brown sugar
16) 6 medium sweet potatoes
17) Directions
1) Peel and slice the potatoes cutting them into ½-inch bits and drop them into a 3 ½-quart Crock-Pot®.

2) In a separate dish, mix the brown sugar, cinnamon, melted butter, and applesauce.

Note: Be sure you pack the brown sugar tight

when it is measured.

3) Empty the mixture over the potatoes in the Pot.

4) When the potatoes are tender; you can top with the chopped nuts. Yummy!

5) *Cooking Time*: Six to Eight hours
6) Sides/Veggies
7) Slow Cooked Baked Potatoes
8) Ingredients
9) 6 Baking Potatoes
10) Kosher Salt
11) Oil
12) Garnishes: Your choice
13) Directions
1) Prepare the potatoes with a good scrub and rinsing, but do not dry them.

2) Put each one in some foil while poking holes in each one using a fork.

3) Use a small amount of oil to drizzle over each one adding a sprinkle of salt, and close the foil.

4) To keep them from getting soggy, ball up

several wads of foil into the cooker.

5) Layer the potatoes on the balls and cover. Leave them on warm in the Crock-Pot® until ready to serve.

6) *Cooking Time*: Low – Six to Eight Hours
7) Corn on the Cob
8) *Ingredients*
9) 3 ears or 5 to 6 halves – Corn on the cob
10) Salt as needed
11) 1/2 stick or ¼ cup of softened butter
12) *Directions*
1) Shuck and remove the silks from the corn; break them into halves.

2) Cover each one with butter and wrap individually in foil.

3) Wad some foil balls up in the base of the unit and add about 1-inch of water.

4) Put the potatoes into the Crock-Pot®, and cook for the allotted time.

5) *Servings*: 4
6) *Preparation Time*: Five minutes
7) *Cooking Time*: Use the high setting for two

hours. *Note*: The cooking time may vary if you prepare the corn with another unit besides a 5 to 6-quart pot.

8) Ranch Mushrooms

9) Ingredients

10) ½ Cup Melted butter

11) 1 Pound fresh mushrooms

12) 1 Package - ranch salad dressing mix

13) Instructions

1) Leave the mushrooms whole and wash them well.

2) Put them into the Crock-Pot®, adding the oil and ranch mix by drizzling it over the mushrooms.

3) Cover the Pot. It is best to stir once after hour one to blend the butter.

4) *Servings*: Six

5) *Cooking Time*: Low will have your mushrooms ready in three to four hours.

6) Sweet Potatoes

7) Ingredients

8) 4 medium sweet potatoes

9) Optional Garnishes:

10) Brown Sugar, Butter, Mini Marshmallows

11) Directions

1) Clean and prepare the potatoes—thoroughly dry.

2) Use a fork and poke holes in each one, and double wrap them in aluminum foil.

3) Put them in the Crock-Pot®--cooking them the specified amount of time. If you are close to the kitchen; turn and flip the potatoes in the pot occasionally.

4) Once they are done, add the garnishes of your choice and serve.

5) *Servings*: Four
6) *Preparation Time*: Five Minutes
7) *Cooking Time*: The Low setting is used for 8 hrs. or the High setting for 4 hrs. (Times may vary depending on the size of the potatoes, but you will know when they are ready by how soft the potato is when you give it a squeeze.)
8)
9)
10)
11)
12)
13)

Chapter 5: Desserts – Snacks & Treats to Devour

Apple Dump Cake

Ingredients
- Butter (1 Stick)
- Yellow cake mix (1 box)
- Apple pie filling (1 Can)

Directions

1) Empty the apple filling into the Crock-Pot®.

2) *Dump* in the mix and then the butter on top of the mix.

3) *Cooking Time*: Cook the cake in the Pot on the low setting for approximately four hours for best results.

4) Enjoy!

Applesauce

Ingredients
- 12 Apples
- 1 teaspoon juice (+) ¼ of the lemon peel
- 2 cinnamon sticks

Directions

1) Peel, core, and slice the apples. Put the apples, lemon peel, and sticks into the Crock-Pot®.

2) Provide a drizzle to the top with the juice and set the cooking timer.

3) When the treat is ready—throw the lemon peel and cinnamon sticks into the garbage.

4) Blend with a regular or immersion blender.

5) Chill for a few hours.

6) *Cooking Time* is five to seven hrs.
7) Peach Cobbler
8) Ingredients
9) 1 White cake mix (not prepared)
10) 6 Large peaches
11) 1- Stick (½- Cup) softened butter
12) Directions
1) Peel and slice the peaches, and put them into the Crock-Pot®.

2) Blend the butter and cake mix using a pastry blender. You want a crumbly texture.

3) Sprinkle the mix over the peaches, and cook.

4) Enjoy with a bowl of ice cream.
5) *Servings*: Eight
6) *Preparation Time*: Fifteen minutes
7) *Cooking Times* on the high setting is two to three hours; whereas the Low cycle will extend for about four hours.
8) Cocktail Franks - Sweet and Sour
9) Ingredients
10) 40- Ounces Pineapple chunks

11) 2 Pounds cocktail franks
12) 1 Cup each:
- Grape jelly

- Chili sauce

- 3 Tablespoons each:
- Prepared mustard

- Lemon juice

- *Directions*
1) Mix the jelly, chili sauce, mustard, and lemon juice in the Pot, mixing it well.

2) Cover and use the high setting for fifteen to twenty minutes to blend the ingredients

3) Slice the franks into bite-sized pieces and add to the Crock-Pot®.

4) Pour in the drained chunks of pineapple.

5) *Servings*: 10
6) *Cooking Times*: *High* setting for two hours; *Low* setting for four hours.
7)

8)
9)
10) Index for the Recipes
11) Chapter 2: Healthy Breakfast Recipes
- Boiled Eggs

- One-Hour Bread

- Breakfast Fiesta Delight

- Italian Sausage Scramble

- **The Sweeter Side of Breakfast**
- Blueberry Steel Cut Oats

- Pumpkin Pie Oatmeal

- Pumpkin Butter

- **Chapter 3: Time-Saving Lunch Specialties**
- Beef Tacos

- Root Beer & BBQ Chicken

- Stuffed Banana Peppers

- Crock-Pot® Taco Soup

- **Chapter 4: Dinner in a Hurry**
- **Beef**
- Meat for the Tacos

- Steak Pizzaiola

- Steak in the Pot

- **Chicken & Turkey**
- Buffalo Chicken

- Caesar Chicken

- Cranberry Chicken

- French Onion Chicken

- Hawaiian Chicken

- Honey Mustard Chicken

- Chicken Italian Style

- Swedish Meatballs

- Sweet and Sour Chicken

- Creamy Taco Chicken

- Stuffed – Roasted Turkey

- **Fish**
- Citrus Flavored Fish

- Salmon Bake

- **Pork**
- BBQ Style Pork Steaks

- Pepsi® Roast

- Ranch Chops

- Ham in Cider Gravy

- **Casseroles**
- Crock-Pot® Dinner: Beef or Chicken

- Squash 'N Chops

- Lasagna Enchantment

- Sweet Potato Casserole

- **Sides & Veggies**
- Slow Cooked Baked Potatoes

- Corn on the Cob

- Ranch Mushrooms

- Sweet Potatoes

- **Chapter 5: Desserts to Devour**
- Apple Dump Cake

- Applesauce

- Peach Cobbler

- Cocktail Franks – Sweet and Sour

-
-
-
-
-

Conclusion

I hope you enjoyed reading through your personal copy of *Crock Pot Mastery Cookbook: The Zero Effort Crock Pot Recipe Guide For Everyone.* Let's hope it was informative and able to provide you with all of the tools you need to achieve your goals. Learning how to cook with your Crock Pot is an easy journey if you have the right tools, and you do!

All you need to do is gather a list and head to the market to get all of the goodies for your newest invention with these 'nifty' recipes. Between your work, children (if you are blessed with them), school and all of the activities involved with life in general, it 's nice to know you can depend on a quick preparation of your meals at the end of a hard day.

www.ingramcontent.com/pod-product-compliance
Lightning Source LLC
LaVergne TN
LVHW010325070526
838199LV00065B/5665